THE LONE WOLF TRADER PRESENTS: MASTERING THE MENTAL GAME

How to overcome the biggest
obstacle to day trading success:
YOURSELF

By Patrick Buchanan

Copyright © 2024 Patrick Buchanan

All rights reserved.

No part of this book may be used or reproduced, distributed, or transmitted in any form or by any means, including photocopying, recording, or other electronic or mechanical methods, without the proper written permission of the publisher, except in the case of brief quotations apart, embodied in critical reviews and certain other non-commercial uses permitted by copyright law. Use of this publication is permitted solely for personal use and must include full attribution of the material's source.

Legal Notice:

This book is copyright protected. This is only for personal use. You cannot amend, distribute, sell, use, quote, or paraphrase any part or the content within this book without the consent of the author.

Disclaimer Notice:

Please note that the information contained within this document is for educational and entertainment purposes only. Every attempt has been made to provide accurate, up-to-date, and reliable complete information. No warranties of any kind are expressed or implied. Readers acknowledge that the author is not engaging in the rendering of legal, financial, medical, or professional advice. The content of this book has been derived from various sources. Please consult a licensed professional before attempting any techniques outlined in this book.

By reading this document, the reader agrees that under no circumstances is the author responsible for any losses, direct or indirect, which are incurred as a result of the use of information contained within this document, including, but not limited to, errors, omissions, or inaccuracies.

| Paperback | ISBN: | 9798333943194 |

TABLE OF CONTENTS

Introduction 7

Chapter One: The Biggest Challenge 16

Chapter Two: Why Is Consistency So Important? 23

Chapter Three: Lack Of Discipline 30

Chapter Four: Being Over Competitive 41

Chapter Five: A Lack Of Perspective 49

Chapter Six: Self-Deception 56

Chapter Seven: Complacency 64

Chapter Eight: Fear 71

Chapter Nine: Greed 80

Chapter Ten: Gluttony 89

Chapter Eleven: Tracking Your Progress 95

Chapter Twelve: Putting The Pieces Together 102

About The Author 111

*A quick housekeeping note before we begin—if you have already read my first book, *"Secrets of the Lone Wolf Trader"* or taken my complete day trading video course, thank you!! I'm confident this book will be a great addition to the concepts you've already learned. If you *haven't* already read my first book or taken my video course, I highly recommend doing that *before* you read this book. It will help lay the foundation that this book builds upon. You can find the book on Amazon, and get my complete video course on my website:

www.lonewolftradingclub.com.

INTRODUCTION

In my first book, "Secrets of the Lone Wolf Trader"—I showed you the specific strategies and techniques I use on a daily basis to trade stock options. That book was more of a 'nuts and bolts' strategy blueprint of the way I personally trade, designed to be easy to understand even for complete beginners. I wanted to teach the same strategy that makes ME over six figures per year *(in just about 5 hours per week)* to people who might have NO experience at all with day trading. That book was a *knowledge-based* book.

THIS book is a *wisdom*-based book. It's designed to help you tackle some of the problems you might face *after* you've already started trading. So, although I feel like this book will be just as quick to read and easy to digest as my first one *(it's definitely shorter)*—unlike the first one, you can't really get the maximum benefit from it if you read this book as an 'absolute beginner'. You should definitely have at least *a little bit* of trading experience under your belt to make the most of it.

One thing that makes writing this book easy is the fact that nearly EVERY trader has gone through many of the same things I'm writing about… so when I'm discussing the most ubiquitous pitfalls you'll encounter, I don't feel like there's a lot of explanation necessary. If you've been trading for any length of time, you've already experienced the things I'm describing. You "get it."

My first book was a *'how to trade'* book, and this one is a *'how to improve your trading'* book. Therefore, a lot of this book will be more esoteric than technical in nature. It won't contain any charts, graphs or technical analysis. But it *will* have plenty of internally facing questions and exercises you can employ to help you overcome the biggest obstacle keeping you from consistent success: *yourself.*

Throughout my life I've been fascinated by everything that has to do with the mind. When I was a teenager, I actually had an interest in becoming a psychologist… and even though I never earned a psychology degree, I do fancy myself an 'armchair psychologist' at this point. What I plan to do with this book is invite you to take a look inward in order to help you determine where you're strong, where you struggle, and how to improve on everything that needs work. Not from a technical perspective *(there are countless "how to trade" books you can read, including MY first book),* but rather from a philosophical perspective.

I believe that many people project their failures onto other people/things and look to 'place the blame' on outside factors that have nothing to do with them. For example, in trading there are so many scapegoats that could shoulder the blame for *your* failures. For example:

> *"Why didn't Powell cut interest rates in today's Fed meeting like everyone thought he would?"*
>
> *"Why didn't this support level hold up like it was supposed to?"*
>
> *"Why didn't this chart pattern work like it was supposed to?"*

And on and on and on.

I have had many days where things happened that *shouldn't have* happened based on my technical analysis. I trust my analysis, and I know it's sound. Does that mean that I need to place blame somewhere else because a particular trade didn't work? I don't think so. I mean, if you're struck by lightning while walking down the street, do you *(assuming you survive)* blame yourself by saying, *"I'm so stupid! Why didn't I just walk on the other side of the street?"* Or do you blame some higher power, looking up at the sky and shouting, *"Why did you try to strike me down, God? I've done nothing but believe in you!"*

Both of those examples sound pretty silly, don't they? Sometimes, *things just happen.* They have no rhyme or reason. They just *are*. It's important to hone your own ability to distinguish between things that happen because of *your own* negligence, and things that *just happen*. "Luck" is a real thing. Good luck, and bad luck. Sometimes your actions have a hand in directing this luck, and sometimes they don't.

My ultimate goal is simply to trade BETTER each and every day. If you've traded at all, you already know that NOTHING is guaranteed in the stock market, and the best you can do is use all of the information available at any time to make the best move based on probabilities.

So how is this book going to improve your trading? First, it's going to prompt you do to a lot of soul searching and self-reflection. I have identified the most common personality traits that can harm any trader on a daily basis— and I'm going to give you some strategies to not only identify why & how they appear, but help you fight them as soon as you see them rearing their ugly heads.

The truth is—we will ALL succumb to some of these negative behaviors at times in our trading journey. Don't beat yourself up if you slip once in a while—just make sure you don't get in the habit of making the same mistakes repeatedly. Remember the old saying: *"Insanity is doing the same thing over and over again and expecting a different result."* Trade sane. Trade controlled. Stay out in front of the trade. Make sure YOU control the trade, rather than the trade controlling you.

Before we get into the heart of the book, there's another thing I want to say right off the bat. Lately *(especially since the AI explosion)* there's been an abundance of apps, indicators and the people pushing these AI apps & indicators promising you huge gains for doing essentially nothing... just, *"Sit back and let the algorithm do the work for you!"*

First of all, I don't believe it. Call me a skeptic, or old fashioned, or whatever. I don't want a computer to make my trading decisions for me just like I don't want a self-driving car. Yes, technology is a huge benefit in many aspects of life... but some things should be left to the humans.

Secondly—for ME, learning how to day trade on my own and then consistently making profits that beat the market day after day—that gives me a HUGE sense of pride. I did that. ME. Not some computer program. I didn't buy my way into some exclusive club *(I started out with about $1,000 in my first trading account)*. I used MY OWN mind, and my own powers of deduction, my own technical analysis skills, my own command of chart awareness and self-discipline, and on and on. The fact that I learned how to do this *all by myself*, and now it's become a six-figure yearly income generator for me—knowing that fact is priceless. I *literally* changed the course of my entire life because of this skill that I learned myself. And you can do the same thing.

ALL of us experience the worst parts of ourselves occasionally. But here's the thing: If you're having a bad day and you act like a dick to a co-worker or the barista at the coffee shop… you'll probably feel bad about it later and wish you had kept your cool. But that slip-up won't cost you hundreds or thousands of dollars… the way it can if you exhibit this type of judgement lapse during trading.

Keeping your wits about you while you trade is one of the MOST important steps in becoming consistently successful. Too many people think more success comes from having more knowledge. *"The more you know, the better you'll trade."* I disagree with this statement. I believe many people become hindered with having *too much information* as they trade. It's the old 'paralysis by analysis' concept rearing its ugly head.

If somebody says to you, *"We can go eat at McDonald's or Burger King. Where do you want to go?"* You'll probably be able to make a split-second decision. But what if they ask a variation of the same question that sounds like this: *"We can go eat at McDonalds, or Burger King, or Wendy's, or KFC, or Arby's, or Sonic, or Chik-Fil-A, or Hardees, or In & Out Burger, or Taco Bell, or Chipotle, or Cava. Where do you want to go?"* Which one of those 2 questions will you be able to answer faster? Exactly. Most of the time, having more information to consider dramatically increases the time it takes you to make a decision. And in day trading, making split-second decisions is absolutely crucial.

That's why, in my opinion, having more *information* about options trading is far less advantageous as having *more control of your emotions* as you trade. The fact is, more often than not you won't fail because you didn't know what you were supposed to do…. You'll fail because although you DID know what you were supposed to do, you didn't *do that thing* because an emotional response kept you from making the right move.

Yes, of course, there are certain technical concepts you MUST have a firm grip on to be consistently successful. Things like knowing how to interpret price action, and identify valid trends, and being able to 'read' the candlesticks as they develop on the chart… but in my opinion, possessing emotional stability and focus as you trade is just as important as anything else.

There's a legendary English band called Throbbing Gristle that was active during the first wave of UK

Punk Rock in the mid-to-late 1970's, and I would guess that 99.9 percent of you reading this book right now would HATE their music *(go listen to a few tracks and see for yourself)*... but I digress. The point is, they have a song called "Discipline" with a bombastic, repetitive lyrical verse that goes: *"Discipline! Discipline! We need some discipline in here!"* I personally love that song, and that verse has become a sort of mantra for me whenever I'm about to do something stupid as I trade. I just imagine the unsettling visage of Genesis P. Orridge screaming at me... *"You need some discipline in here!!!"*

I bring up discipline because that was *my* biggest problem when I was a beginner, and so that one definitely hits close to home. There are plenty of detrimental behaviors that can trip you up on a daily basis as you trade, but in my opinion, these are the TOP 8 offenders:

1. Lack of discipline

2. Being over competitive

3. Lack of perspective

4. Self-deception

5. Complacency

6. Fear

7. Greed

8. Gluttony

I'm just going to put this out there right now: I believe that FEAR and GREED are the 2 most destructive behaviors on this list, but *all* of them can wreak havoc on your trading if left unchecked. Throughout this book I'm going to explain why I believe all of these are extremely detrimental, how you can tell if you have succumbed to any of them, and if so—what you can do to change it. Every behavior is learned, and therefore can be un-learned… so if you find yourself making self-destructive moves on the regular—just identify exactly ***what*** you are doing wrong, then identify ***why*** you're making those incorrect moves, and then identify ***how*** you can un-learn the behaviors that put you on the destructive path in the first place. Identifying **WHAT>WHY>HOW.** That's the blueprint for success, and that's what I'm going to teach you in this book. Are you ready? Let's go!

CHAPTER ONE:
THE BIGGEST CHALLENGE

You've probably heard people say, *"It's so hard to make money in the stock market!"* That's the furthest thing from the truth. It's incredibly easy to make money in the stock market every day. BUT... it's also incredibly easy to LOSE money in the market every day. You know what's NOT incredibly easy? Being ***consistently profitable.***

That's right. Being consistently profitable is the biggest challenge for EVERY trader, whether they're trading a $1,000 account or a $100,000 account. Every trader has winning trades and losing trades. I mean, you could decide whether to go long or short on the day by flipping a coin, and you'd be right 50% of the time. But being consistently profitable, day after day— *that's* the thing that separates the professionals from the amateurs. That's what you want, and that's the hardest thing to achieve. So that's our main goal, and the focus of this book:

HELPING YOU ACHIEVE CONSISTENT DAY TRADING PROFITABILITY BY IDENTIFYING AND ELIMINATING DESTRUCTIVE BEHAVIORS.

The thing that keeps you from being consistently profitable in your trading isn't the market 'faking you out', or price slippage on your options contracts, or your technical analysis not being correct *(although all of those things **can** negatively affect you and **do** happen)*... it's your own destructive behaviors.

Most of the time this isn't an intellectual problem, it's an emotional one. More often than not it's not a lack of knowledge, but rather a lack of discipline or emotional development that trips traders up.

I plan on identifying some of the most consequential mistakes you can make in your trading, help you determine why you're making those mistakes, and give you some techniques you can use to stop those mistakes from happening. Trading is both an art and a science, and it's important to remember both the 'art' and 'science' part of it as you navigate through the day.

The ART side of trading involves seeing the charts and candlesticks for what they really are, not what you *want* them to show you based on a preconceived bias. It also involves being able to predict price action movements on multiple time frames and take advantage of that ability. For example, being able to see an opportunity on the immediate time frame and scalp it for a win, while also being able to see a longer-term play setting up. It's basically the day trading version of playing "3D chess" instead of checkers.

The SCIENCE part of it involves paying attention to things like time until expiration *(how you manage a trade needs to change depending on how much time is left until your options expire),* understanding the Greeks *(specifically Delta and Theta, which are in my opinion the 2 most important ones),* and all of the other things that relate to the numbers rather than the candlesticks or chart patterns. You can't just consider one or the other. You need to take both art and science into consideration. But this isn't a trading guide: it's a mental strategy manual. I'm not going to 'teach you how to trade' in this book. If you want to learn exactly how I trade, step by step: get my first book, *"Secrets of the Lone Wolf Trader"* which *does* teach you how to trade. THIS book is all about 'getting your mind right.'

So, back to consistency. Why is it THE most important thing in day trading? Because I'm assuming you want to actually do this for more than a few weeks or months, right? I've been day trading full time for years, and I plan to do this until the day I die. The only reason I *can* plan on doing this forever is because I have achieved consistency. If you are not consistently successful you WILL blow up your account, and then you're finished for good. Time to go get another job working for someone else. I know that sounds like fear-mongering hyperbole, but it's the truth. A majority of day traders simply don't succeed in the long run. I believe the MAIN reason most traders fail is because they focus on the PROFITS over the CONSISTENCY.

If the most important thing to you is the size of the wins, you've thrown yourself off track before you even get anywhere. You're trying to get to point C while skipping point B. Here's how it *should* work:

> **Point A:** You are a fresh-faced newbie excited to change your life through day trading.
>
> **Point B:** You are perfectly happy to trade *small* size and make *small* daily gains in order to get more experience under your belt each day each day, therefore getting more comfortable with the process without risking too much.
>
> **Point C:** You have proven to yourself that you know what you're doing, and NOW you're ready to slowly scale up.

The 'scaling up' part is where you'll actually make

REAL money. I make *(on average)* between $2,000 to $4,000 each day now, but I trade a LOT of contracts each day. You simply cannot expect to make 3K per day trading 3 contracts. I mean, it's *possible*... but the odds of it happening are long. You'd need some sort of extreme catalyst or 'black swan' type of event to make it happen... and it's *certainly* not predictable.

What I do is predictable price action trend trading, day after day. Simply looking at the same tickers each and every day, with nothing 'special' happening on the day... this approach is just me looking at the chart, playing the chart, and using enough size to actually make real money. The type of thing you can do day after day, with nothing more to it than analyzing the chart patterns and the candlesticks.

Sounds simple, right? Here's where things get tricky. It's easy enough to know what you *should* do in any given situation, but it's a lot harder to actually *do* the right thing, for a variety of different reasons I'll cover in the book. The reason why this book is all about mental focus and attitude is because I believe that getting your mental game right is actually a LOT harder than simply creating a trading strategy.

To be perfectly honest, you don't need to be dazzlingly smart to be able to trade successfully. Yes, of course intelligence helps *(just like in every other aspect of life)*, but knowledge and intelligence are not the most important things. Having control of your own emotions IS the most important thing. To be able to do that ONE thing you know you should do, when all of your emotions are begging you to do the other thing. Realizing 'the thing you should do' is the knowledge part of the process... but being able to *actually do it* is the emotional discipline part of it—and that part is MUCH harder.

Back when I was BRAND NEW to trading most of my losses were due to simply not having enough knowledge. But over the last few years, every single loss I've had was because I failed to do the thing I knew I should do... because one or more emotional hangups kept me from doing that thing. I imagine most other traders have had similar problems as they've evolved. Each one of us is navigating individual minefields full of unique challenges as we trade, but there are certain things that are 'constants' on that minefield. My goal in writing this book is to identify the biggest offenders, help you see which ones are affecting *you* the most, and give you some ideas of how to stop them.

Ultimately, we all want the same thing: MONEY. But the 'correct' way to get that money through day trading is to focus on the processes that will get you that money, meaning: consistency in your trades. With consistency comes money. So,

CONSISTENCY=MONEY. You should shift your thinking from, *"I want money"* to, *"I want to be a consistent trader".*

The ESSENTIAL first step is buying into the concept of: **CONSISTENCY IS MORE IMPORTANT THAN PROFIT.** Once you've done that, the profits will follow.

CHAPTER TWO: WHY IS CONSISTENCY SO IMPORTANT?

As I mentioned in the last chapter: being consistent is literally *the one thing* that can guarantee your ability to stay in the trading game over the long haul. Think about it. When you are *not* consistently profitable, that means you might have one nice, juicy green day where you make 1 or 2K on the day… but then the next day you'll lose $600, and the day after that you'll lose $500, or $700… and before you know it, you've just given back all of the profits you made on that big fat green day, the one you were so excited to tell everyone about. If you're experiencing these "roller coaster" swings in your daily P&L, you're much more likely to blow up your account.

But when you ARE consistent—you're growing

the account, day after day after day. Your daily profits might be $100, or they might be $1,000, but that's not the point. The point is—*whatever* those profits are, they're happening each and every day, and your account gets bigger day after day. It's like a slow, consistent snowball rolling downhill and picking up size along the way. Sure, it's NOT as 'sexy' as winning in some super risky trade that nets you 200% P&L in 1 hour, but it's a thing you CAN do day after day.

Anyone who claims that you can consistently hit those *"to the moon"* trades is lying to you. Sure, anyone *can* potentially hit trades like that—but can you count on doing it with consistency and predictability? NOPE. But can you count on small, yet consistently green P&L? That IS absolutely doable. I've been trading for many years now, and I've never blown up an account. The largest loss I've had on any single trade was roughly $5,000, and that hurt A LOT. It was at that moment that I took a long, hard look at myself in the mirror, and decided I had 2 options: either quit trading for good or make *massive* changes to the way I approached my own trading. You know which path I chose, and here we are.

Before I continue, let's talk about what I actually mean when I say 'consistency'. That term *(in relation to day trading)* can mean different things to different people—but for ME, consistency simply means being right MORE OFTEN than being wrong—and having your profits on your winning days be MORE than the losses on your losing days.

A trader who has three of five days GREEN for the week, with their winning days averaging $300 per day and their losses averaging $100 per day IS *consistent*.

A trader who has one GREEN day in the week, with a profit of $600, and four RED days with losses averaging $100 per day is NOT consistent. It doesn't matter that they still posted a $200 overall profit on the week.

Being *profitable* and being *consistent* are not the same thing.

I'm not a huge sports fan, but I'm about to make a sports analogy here, simply because it fits this scenario very well. In football, you've probably heard the saying, *"Defense wins championships."* The defensive part of the game is decidedly less sexy and less dramatic that it's offensive counterpart. Everyone would rather see an 80-yard touchdown pass than watch a guy get tackled for a 1-yard gain. But the statement is true. A team that has a flashy offense *without* a rock-solid defense is probably not winning many championships.

In trading, most people like to focus on their daily profits *(in a dollar amount)* or on their P&L *(in a percentage amount)*. This is essentially 'the offense' in trading. What's less talked about and adored is the day-after-day wins, even if they're not as dramatic. This is 'the defense' in trading. Most people would rather say, *"I made 5K today!"* Even though they lost $600 the day before, and $800 the day before that… than say, *"I've made $100 a day for the past 2 weeks straight!"* It simply *sounds* sexier to talk about a 5K haul. But just because it sounds sexier does NOT make it more important. Yes, obviously you want to eventually get to those 5K days, but you need to do it the right way—calculated, strategic, taking every shot with intention and focus—rather than a 'throw everything at the wall and see what sticks' approach that comes from having the lack of a defined strategy.

I guarantee you—at the end of the month, the trader with a month of consistent $100 days will be far ahead of the rollercoaster trader that has the occasional 1K day interspersed with hundreds of dollars in losses on the days before or after that 1K day. It's the 'tortoise and the hare' story come to life.

So back to the question, *"Why is consistency so important?"* Helping you achieve consistency day after day by upping the level of your *mental game* is the main reason I'm writing this book. In one sentence, here is the summary of what I aim to teach you in this book: **I want to show you how you can identify and eliminate negative thought patterns and/or**

behaviors that keep you from being consistently profitable in your trades.

As you'll see when we get further into the book: there are many different ways you can get 'tripped up', and not every negative thought/behavior affects each of us the same way. The things that tripped ME up might not affect you at all—and likewise, the things YOU struggle with might have little to no impact on ME. The important part is being honest with yourself when you take that long, hard look in the mirror.

I can tell you everything you *should* do to become more consistently successful in your trading, if you are honest with yourself.... But I CAN'T MAKE YOU BE HONEST WITH YOURSELF. Only *you* can do that. So don't sell yourself short. You've already taken the first step, because you're reading this book right now. Don't be afraid to go all the way and really look into the depths of your psyche and your soul. That's the only way you'll discover the true answers you're looking for.

Just like I can't *make you* be honest with yourself, I can't *make you* do any of the exercises I suggest in this book. I can show you what to look out for and tell you how you can improve certain aspects of your trading by doing these exercises—but I can't be there to slap your hand away from the mouse when you're about to do something stupid. Trading is ALL ABOUT personal responsibility, self-reflection and honesty—being honest with yourself. None of us are perfect, and whenever you're critiquing yourself, it's simply impossible to be 100% objective. But you WANT to be as objective as possible, always. The closer to 'pure objectivity' you can get while critiquing yourself, your strengths and flaws—the quicker you can improve on all of the things that need work.

Here's one thing I want you to start doing immediately, if you're not already doing it. Each day, write down the amount of your daily P&L in both percentage AND dollar amounts. Since your P&L can dramatically change based on how many contracts you trade each day, make sure you keep your trading size fairly constant for a period of time *(preferably at least one month)*. So, if your goal is to trade approximately $1,000 per day in total, don't decide to trade $200 one day and $2,000 the next day. Yes, you can scale up or down each day based on what's happening on the charts, because some days are simply less conducive to trading with my strategy *(for example, consolidation days with a lot of sideways price action)*... but try not to make your sizing dramatically different from day to day.

You want to give yourself a baseline to start from. Once you know how your average performance is trading 1K each day, then when you decide to increase your daily capital investment to 2 or 3K, you've got the numbers to compare it to. The less variables you have to consider, the more you can chalk-up your success or failure to your own actions. If you trade $100 one day and $3,000 the next day, of course your results will be wildly different each day, but you won't be as certain what was the *cause* of that difference. If you trade approximately $1,000 per day *(or $300, or whatever number you want to start with)*. When you trade with approximately the same amount each day for weeks or months, it's more like an 'apples to apples' comparison rather than an 'apples to oranges' one.

I can't stress this enough: **CONSISTENCY IS THE KEY TO YOUR SUCCESS.** If you can be consistently successful, you WILL be able to do this for the long haul. If you *can't* be consistent, you will eventually blow up your account. If that thought scares you, good. It *should* scare you. Once you blow up the account, it's game over. So, make SURE that the most important thing on your mind is achieving consistency. NOT huge dollar profits or massive P&L. Simple consistency. Even if it's small. Be happy with smaller profits *at first,* knowing those profits will slowly get bigger over time.

CHAPTER THREE:
LACK OF DISCIPLINE

Anyone can exhibit one or more of the negative behaviors I discuss in this book, but every trader will have that one *'Achilles heel'* behavior that really trips them up on a daily basis- the one that affects them more than the others. It's different for everyone. The one specific thing that trips *you* up might not affect the next trader at all.

For *me,* lack of discipline has always been MY *'Achilles heel'*. It's been the main reason for all of my biggest losses, and the thing I've worked on the MOST regarding my own trading. My problem was never a lack of knowledge, or bad technical analysis… it was a lack of discipline that would cause me to get into situations I never should have gotten into. Going too big when I should have scaled it back, or keeping a trade open longer than I should have, because the optimist in me just believed it would come back, even though it didn't… things like that.

In my case, this is because I've always had a wild spirit. If you read my first book, you know I'm a lifelong musician, the son of an artist… I've lived a very 'free' life, basically doing whatever the hell I wanted to do in most situations, regardless of the consequences. The way my brain is hardwired can cause me to be a bit reckless. I'm not afraid of many things, and I'm not greedy…therefore, *FEAR and GREED* have rarely affected my trades. But I AM undisciplined. So, for ME, while fear and greed might not be a thing, lack of discipline definitely *was* a thing.

Here's one subtle distinction that can be a bit tricky to navigate: determining the difference between trading *aggressively* and trading *recklessly*. Trading aggressively is perfectly acceptable. It's something I do all the time. In fact, I'm FAR more likely to be very aggressive than conservative in my trading. But there's a fine line between having courage in the trade and having a lack of self-discipline.

There's calculated risk, and then there's undisciplined risk. Here's a 'real world' example of this: Let's say you want to go out walking around the city for the day. The weather forecast says there's a 20% chance of rain. You don't want to bring an umbrella, because carrying an umbrella all day is a pain in the ass. You have an 8 out of 10 chance it will NOT rain on you. Therefore, in this case, your decision to not take the umbrella is a calculated risk. *Chances are*, it will not rain on you, and you're willing to accept those odds.

But what if the weather forecast says there's an 80% chance of rain? In this case, deciding to NOT take the umbrella is an undisciplined risk. *Chances are*, it's going to rain on you, and then it will really suck to walk around the city soaking wet all day because you didn't bring an umbrella.

Trading ALWAYS involves risk. If you are not willing to accept risk, you should NOT even consider trading *(unless you never move beyond paper trading, and what's the point of that?)* The important thing is to be able to tell the difference between calculated risk and undisciplined risk. I actually consider myself to be fairly 'risky' with a lot of the moves I make—but my risks are *always* calculated ones, never undisciplined. It wasn't always this way, but with a lot of personal work and self-reflection I've been able to hone my abilities to do a better job of telling the difference between the two.

Calculated risks are perfectly acceptable. Undisciplined risks are not. Be able to tell the difference in your trades.

When you're aggressive, you make your moves

with an end goal in mind. There's a strategy and a process to the whole thing: so even when a trade is losing you money that very minute, it's OK because in the grand scheme of things you still have confidence in your original trade idea. Trading with a lack of discipline means you'll see half-baked setups and jump in anyway, because you can't help yourself. The aggressive trader takes risks when they see a defined end goal in mind. The reckless trader has no end goal, they just want to feel the excitement of being in the trade 'just because'. The reckless trader is more of an adrenaline junkie than a technician. I'm a technician. I never roll the dice just to roll the dice.

What are some signs that you have a lack of discipline?

1. Letting your need for excitement overshadow your technical analysis

This is classic *"YOLO!"* behavior. When your need to just *feel the excitement* of being in the trade takes precedence over what your technical analysis is actually telling you. There IS a time and place to go big and REALLY lay some size into a trade. Don't think that you *always* need to be super careful and conservative. But at the same time, you can't throw the kitchen sink at every single trade. Doing that is the quickest way to blow up your account. If you find yourself frequently going too big, too quickly—that's a sign that you need to work on your discipline.

Let your level of confidence in a trade determine the size you work with. If my technical analysis says there's a 'decent' chance a trade will work out, I might put small size on it. When my technical analysis says there's a 'highly probable' chance a trade will work out, I'm happy putting a lot more size on it. I might be equally excited about both trades, but I will size each one according to what my technical analysis is telling me.

2. Stopping yourself out before you should

This shows a lack of discipline *(and also crosses into 'fear' territory)*. When you know what you're doing, you should be able to create your own support and resistance levels. If you're reading this book, I assume you're not a 'complete beginner', and I trust that you DO know how to plot your own support/resistance levels. If you don't already know how to do this, it's something you should definitely learn *before* you place another trade. It's an absolutely essential skill. I would say being able to interpret the price action movement of the candlesticks is THE most important day trading skill to have, followed closely by the ability to identify valid support & resistance levels. You MUST learn how to do both of these things if you want to achieve consistency.

So, first you need to develop the ability to draw valid support & resistance levels, but then you need to actually *trust your levels*. When you know what you're doing, most of the time your levels *(or the area close to your levels)* WILL be valid. Trust yourself and your technical analysis. What that means is—if price is working against you but it still has some room to move before it touches your stop out level—DON'T close early just because it's scary to see some red on your P&L. Frequently a trade will be red before it's green. Trades don't always go in our favor from open to close. Sometimes they take a detour and wander off in directions we wish they didn't go… but that's life. Identify your absolute line in the sand level, and DON'T stop out of the trade until it breaks that level.

Remember, you must exercise extreme discipline whether you are winning OR losing. When you're winning, discipline means taking profits on big pushes, never getting greedy, never holding longer than you should. The chart will tell you when it's time to get out of the position. For example, let's say you're in long and price has been steadily rising all morning, but then we're coming up on a resistance level AND price is starting to plateau at the same time, instead of the consistent trending movement it was making earlier. Logic tells you that THIS is probably a good time close out your remaining contracts, or at the very least size down a lot. You should have already been paying yourself by closing out contracts over time on big pushes. This is really the heart of my strategy- getting in at the start of a trend, riding the trend while it has maximum steam, closing contracts one by one on big pushes, and then GETTING OUT before the trend loses steam.

When you're losing, discipline means staying in the trade until it breaks your absolute level. But it ALSO means actually getting out once it *does* break that level. Too many traders will have their stop out levels broken, but think, *"Just a few more minutes, and price will come back in my favor."* When you think like this, more often than not you'll end up losing even more money than you would have if you had just stopped out at the level you set for yourself at the beginning. The levels are there for a reason: when you possess the required self-discipline you can actually *respect* your levels.

Some exercises to improve your discipline:

1. Start SMALL, and only add in when price action has proven it's safe to add in

One of the most important trading techniques you should be using ALL THE TIME is: never get in with 100% of your size right away. Put out some feelers and see if your initial inclination was correct. If it WAS correct, then you can add in with more size once price action has confirmed that you were right from the beginning.

As a general rule, I like to limit myself to 10% of my total daily trading size with each entry. For example: if I plan on only trading 10 contracts total on that day, I will only allow myself to purchase ONE contract at a time *(10% of my total involvement)*. If I was planning on trading 20 contracts total on the day, I might let myself get in with 2 contracts at once. 30 contracts total on the day, I would let myself buy 3 contracts at once. You get the picture. This way, you're never getting in over your head with too much size on each entry before you've proven to yourself that the trade is actually working.

It's very tempting to go all-in as soon as you see the start of a big move. But the closer to the beginning of a real move you are, the higher probability there is for a fake out to happen. It's incredibly frustrating to go in with huge size, only to see a huge candle in the wrong direction form the next minute. For example, if you're planning on trading 10 contracts total—when you see the beginning of a trend forming—instead of opening 10 contracts, open ONE, and give it a few minutes to see if it's working. If the trend IS working for you, add in with one more a few minutes later when you see a slight dip. And then of course you'll close contracts on big pushes in your favor, while ALSO adding in on slight dips. This way, you'll be 'playing the chart' like an instrument, rather than throwing everything at the trade at one time.

2. Give yourself self-imposed limitations, and stick to them

NOT allowing yourself to make particular moves will develop your self-discipline. Like forcing yourself to NOT place any trades until 10 minutes into the morning session or forcing yourself to only trade one contract at a time, even though you *could* trade 50 contracts at once if you wanted to. Or forcing yourself to take profits when you've made X amount of profit, even though you want to stay in. I'm NOT saying you should *always* wait 10 minutes before you get into any trade *(or do any of the other exercises I'll describe in this book)*... I'm just saying that IF having self-discipline is a problem for you, these exercises could help you out, as will the exercises in the other chapters.

One thing that helped me out immensely was when I gave myself a time limit on my daily entries. I trade in the mornings, and most of the real price action volatility happens during the first hour of the day- so I made myself refrain from getting IN after 1 hour. That's not saying that I made myself open AND close all contracts within the hour- I will frequently go into the afternoon or swing the trade overnight *(and sometimes even for a few days)*, but I will stop myself from opening any NEW positions after 60 minutes is up. This keeps me from falling for a lot of half-baked price action movements that can act as 'fake outs' after the first 60 minutes of the day.

At the core of what 'discipline' means: it's NOT letting yourself do everything you want. You might *want to* jump into every trade that looks exciting or promising... but *should you* really? You might *want to* add back into the trade that's already worked three times this morning, but *should you?* Of course, all of this is situational. There are particular instances where maybe price is just ripping all day long and you can keep going back to the well endlessly that day. But most of the time, a big move will have a limited time frame for it to work.

3. Avoid letting financial news stories color your analysis

It's nearly impossible to *not* pay any attention to the news. We're bombarded by news from social media, friends and family, etc. SOME of these news stories have actual merit, and it's definitely a skill in itself to be able to separate valid information from fluff. But remember this: a journalist's goal isn't to help you make better trades. It's to help themselves get clicks.

Let's say we have 2 identical news stories about a

potential pullback in the market in the coming months. The first one has this headline:

A POSSIBLE MARKET CORRECTION COULD BE ON THE HORIZON

And the other one has this headline:

TIME TO PANIC? SIGNS WARN OF AN IMPENDING BEAR MARKET

Which one do you think gets more clicks? Obviously the second headline, and the writers realize this. Headlines are structured to tug at your emotions, not engage with your intellect *(I should know… I wrote advertising copy for years, and I'm still writing at this very moment!)* :)

The point is—every news story contains information that might be useful, or might *not* be useful. It's easy to fall into the trap of reading a news story and then making moves based on what you just read in the story. If you do this, you are exhibiting a lack of discipline. It's OK to stay abreast of what's happening, but remember: the charts that *you studied with your own eyes* should direct your actions, not some story written by somebody you don't know.

CHAPTER FOUR:
BEING OVER COMPETITIVE

In America, the need to constantly WIN no matter what is something that's been ingrained into many of us since childhood. Whether it's in sports, or business, or school, the idea that *"If you ain't first you're last"* is always lurking at the back of our brains. In general terms, I don't have a problem with this. I mean, having a strong competitive spirit is obviously preferable to being complacent and lazy. But there IS a point in trading when the *"Win at all costs"* attitude can bite you in the ass. Why is that?

Because the need to always *win* will make you stay in losing trades longer than you should. It will keep you from simply *accepting* the fact that a particular trade DIDN'T work. Accepting defeat. That is something that is VERY difficult for a lot of people to do. And it's easy to understand why. We all hate to lose. I *definitely* hate to lose, but I never let my competitive side cloud my judgement about what is actually happening on the charts right in front of my eyes.

There's the thing that we WANT to happen, and there's the thing that actually IS happening. Sometimes they're the same, but sometimes not. And when your competitive nature is too strong, it won't allow you to see what *is actually* happening. You'll remain myopically committed to your original plan even after the point when it's completely illogical to stay in a trade. I have been guilty of this before. I almost never fall victim to this behavior now, but back when I was a beginning trader there were many times when I'd be losing and say to myself *"This HAS to turn around"*… as if you could just 'gut it out' in a trade the way an MMA fighter can sometimes just win on heart alone. It simply doesn't work like that.

Be OK with losing. Don't let the "loser" stigma paralyze you. EVERYONE loses sometimes. I'm green about 80% of the time, and I'm a successful day trader with NO other job. This is how I make 100% of my income. And guess what? I'm a LOSER 20% of the time… and that's fine with me! I've got nothing to prove to anyone. The only proof I need is in my bank account.

I often say things like, *"be in the now"* and, *"just trade the chart that's right in front of you"*, and I do believe all of those things. But sometimes it's good to focus on the future… specifically when it comes to being over-competitive. Because if you're over-competitive, *everything* feels like 'life or death'. It's hard for a person who thinks like this to just realize that there's always tomorrow, and the next day, and the day after that. Just because you're not winning TODAY doesn't mean you can't win TOMORROW.

What are some signs that you're being over-competitive in your trading?

1. Having unrealistic P&L goals.

This problem stems from having a bit of 'self-delusion', meaning- If you've bought ONE contract, you can't expect that one contract to make you thousands of dollars in one day *(unless you're trading a very expensive ticker and it's also a huge day for that ticker)*.

If I go to the basketball court and practice my jump shot for an hour each day, it's realistic to think that by next month my jump shot will be a lot better than it is now. It's NOT realistic to think that I'll be playing in the NBA next month. Being 'naturally competitive' makes us think we'll always find some way to pull out the win, no matter what happens. But when your level of competitiveness clouds your judgement about what's *actually realistic,* it's a problem.

I can think of many trades I took back when I was an inexperienced trader- and when I review some of the things I did, I can't believe how stupid I was. A lot of these stupid moves originated from the fact that I just couldn't admit to myself that I was WRONG in my analysis, or my timing, or both. I was so eager to "know what I was doing" that I couldn't admit to myself when I *didn't* know what I was doing, and that cost me. I have had a few trades where I lost over $1,000 on one ticker over the course of a few days. This would NEVER happen to me now.

That same move that *(back then)* cost me over $1,000 and a few days of holding would NOW be a one- or two-hundred-dollar loss in the course of ONE day. Why? Because I'm OK with being WRONG now, so I don't feel the need to hold on for dear life to every trade until it works. I'm OK with losing. In the long run, as long as the frequency and the P&L amount of your losses is *less than* the frequency and P&L amount of your wins- then those losses are basically inconsequential. It's not like we're talking about the difference between being UP $3,000 on the week or being DOWN $3,000 on the week—we're talking about the difference between being up $3,000 or being up $3,500.

2. Having a problem accepting defeat

Once again, the "win at all costs" attitude helps fuel

this destructive behavior. I've said this over and over, in my first book, in my video course and on my YouTube channel—*"don't trade scared, and don't trade greedy"*... but there's a fine line between NOT trading scared and being too stubborn for your own good. And that 'fine line' is actually your technical analysis—more specifically, your support & resistance levels. This is why it's so important to REALLY hone your technical analysis skills, and then trust your levels once you set them. When you set your stop-out level and price crosses above or below that level *(telling you it's time to stop out for a loss)* don't say to yourself, *"Let me give it just a little more time"*. Stop out, take the loss and live to trade another day.

YES, there will be some instances when the minute after you stop out for a loss the price reverses, going back in the direction you wanted it to go in the first place. That WILL happen, and when that happens, it's a shitty feeling. But the fact is—if your support & resistance levels were set correctly, when the price does cross over your stop-out threshold, MOST of the time it will keep going in that direction for a while, at least long enough to *really* eat into your position had you left it open. So, for each trade that *would have* made you your money back had you stayed in, there will be 8-9 times that it just keeps going, and every additional minute you stay in, you lose more money.

Remember—in trading, nothing is guaranteed… so the best thing you can do is ask yourself, "What's the most likely thing to happen in this situation?" After you answer that question for yourself, *trust* the answer, and make your moves based on that answer. When the most likely thing to happen is that you will continue to lose if you stay in a position, simply get out and accept the loss. The only time there's 'no tomorrow' is if you blow up your account, so avoiding THAT should *absolutely* be the most important thing to you on a daily basis.

What are some techniques you can implement to avoid being over-competitive in your trading?

1. Remember that this is a marathon and NOT a sprint.

You should never try to 'get rich quick' with your trades. Don't say to yourself, *"I NEED to make $1,000 today!"* Instead, say to yourself, *"I'm going to focus on trading as perfectly as I can today."* That first sentence focuses on making money, while the second sentence focuses on doing whatever is best for the trade. Sometimes, what's best for the trade is actually losing, if that loss keeps you from an *even bigger* loss. When you're OK with losing, you can exit the trade with a *small* loss, focus your attention elsewhere to other tickers, and keep trading.

2. Stop focusing on making money—focus on trading well instead.

Obviously, we all want to make money by day trading. But it's especially dangerous to focus solely on the profits when you have that hyper-competitive streak. Don't trade to make money. Trade to trade well. If you focus on trading well, the money will come. But if you focus on making money *over* trading well, you'll take unnecessary risks that will hurt you.

3. Realize that your only competition is yourself

If you watch my YouTube channel, or follow any other full-time traders' social media channels, you'll see all of the success stories we share. It can be easy to feel that FOMO and say to yourself, *"How come this guy is so successful and I'm trying to trade the same way, but it's not working for me?"* The first problem here is: you can't compare yourself to anyone else. Not people who are more successful than you, and not people who are less successful than you. NOBODY. The ONLY person you should be comparing yourself to is the trader that *you* were last month, or last week, or yesterday. Are YOU doing better now than YOU were doing last week? If so, that's a win. If not, it's time to look inside and do some soul searching.

Everyone is different. Your life story, goals, challenges, availability of capital and risk tolerance is different than everyone else's. The over-competitive streak that whispers in your ear, *"You need to be better than that guy"* is a destructive force. You don't really *know* me *(or any other pro traders)*. You can't compare yourself to someone you don't know. But you do know *yourself*, or at least you *should* know yourself. And if you've suddenly realized that you don't really 'know yourself' in regard to your own trading style, no worries—that's what I'm trying to help you do in this book!

CHAPTER FIVE:
A LACK OF PERSPECTIVE

What does having a 'lack of perspective' while trading mean? This one is a bit harder to describe than the other chapters in this book. It's easy to identify how fear or greed affect your trades, but lack of perspective is a bit more open to interpretation. For me, having a lack of perspective means simply losing your 'place in space', so-to-speak. Where you are in 'the grand scheme' of your trading journey. Remember, we're all on a journey, and we're all at different points in our journey.

Think about this: on any given day there are many people attempting to climb Mt. Everest. One person might be just above base camp, while someone else is near the summit. One person is a first timer, and the other one has already reached the summit and they're back for another try. Both of these people are climbing the same mountain at the same time, but they're both at very different points on their journey. It's like this in trading. Having the proper perspective means being able to realize your place in space and see things as they really *are*, rather than how you want them to be. Having a realistic idea of what to expect from your trades each day, rather than a 'fantasy' perspective.

Having this 'proper perspective' will allow you to take on the correct sizing in your trades, set the correct stop loss levels and target P&L levels, and be satisfied with what you make each day based on your sizing.

For example: If you're trading ONE contract that cost you $100, you shouldn't think that you can hold on until you've made $1,000 that same day. This type of thinking is simply unrealistic. Anything over a 10% P&L on the day can be considered *good*, and 10% on $100 is $10. So, if you trade one $100 contract and you make $30 in one day, you're actually doing REALLY good! Thinking that you can make 1K on one inexpensive options contract in one day shows a lack of perspective.

Another behavior that shows a lack of perspective is when you trade just for the sake of trading, without a strategy or a goal. Being in it *just to be in it*. It's important to know what to look out for, and refrain from jumping into the market until you actually SEE it. I'm not saying you need to get SUPER granular, like—*"I need to see a double-bottom that bounces off the 200 EMA before I go long"*… but just make sure you see *something* that gives you the confidence to take a specific action, whether it's a particular pattern setting up, or the movement on the candlesticks, a support or resistance level that gets broken, or something else entirely.

Understanding what's possible *(and probable)* within a particular time frame is also extremely important. Failure to understand time 'in the right way' shows a lack of perspective. For example, if AAPL is trading just under $200 per share, and you bought out of the money call options at a $210 strike price—if you have ONE DAY of time left until expiration, it's virtually impossible that your options will expire ITM. But if you have ONE MONTH until expiration, it's entirely possible that those options would be ITM by the time they expire. Of course, they would also cost a lot more per contract *(because of the extra time until expiration)*.

TIME EQUALS MONEY, both in the cost of the options and the amount of Theta decay you'll experience at the expiry approaches. There's no 'absolute' right or wrong way to trade in regard to strike prices and expiry dates—you can combine them however you'd like. Not all combinations will give you the same results, but as long as you follow my core strategy *(staying on the RIGHT side of a strong trend)* and understand when to enter and exit—you'll most likely profit, whether your expiry is tomorrow or next month. Just make sure you really understand the connection between time and money when it comes to strike prices and expiration dates. I won't get into that here *(I covered all of that in my first book).*

What are some signs that you're not seeing 'the bigger picture' when you trade?

1. Having unrealistic P&L expectations related to the number of contracts you're holding

I touched on this already in this chapter. Being realistic means understanding what is actually possible, versus the daydreams you have in your mind. Of course, we all want every trade to give us 100%+ P&L, and we want to watch everything go to the moon the second we hit 'buy'… but that is simply not realistic.

Be OPTIMISTIC *and* REALISTIC at the same time. Always believe that you will succeed in the trade, but never let your own perspective on the trade wander into 'pie in the sky' territory.

2. Thinking that you're ready to 'size up' before you are ACTUALLY ready to size up

I was guilty of this many times when I was starting out. I would have one really good week of solid green days *(trading small size)* and then think to myself, *"I'm ready to trade up! Massive gainzzz, here I come!"* Only to lose a huge amount of money the very first day I DID size up. At the time, I simply wasn't ready to handle the extra size yet. It's like an 8-year-old trying to wear a teenager's shoes... they simply don't fit yet. My lack of perspective made me think I was ready to take on the extra size when I wasn't.

The fact is: whenever you trade a significantly larger number of contracts than when you're used to trading, many aspects of the experience will feel completely different. The fluctuation in your P&L *(both positive and negative)* will be a LOT more pronounced with a larger number of contracts. You might be completely comfortable seeing moves of plus or minus $50 in the course of a few minutes. But are you comfortable seeing a plus or minus move of $500 in a few minutes? That's the type of difference you'll see when you size up. I definitely DO encourage everyone to size up eventually *(if you don't size up at a certain point, then you're just being complacent)*... just be prepared for what awaits you when you eventually do size up.

Some exercises to improve your perspective:

1. Don't focus on your profits as a dollar amount- focus on your P&L as a percentage. Like I said earlier in this chapter: A 10% gain on the day is a good P&L... but 10% of $200 is $20. Saying *"I made $20 today trading"* is a lot less impressive than saying *"I made 10% on my P&L today."* When you're starting out you should be trading SMALL, like one contract per day to start. You can get plenty of options contracts on different tickers that run between $100-$200 per contract for an IN THE MONEY contract.

I normally only trade slightly IN the money or AT the money options contracts. I never buy far OUT of the money contracts, because obviously, the further out of the money you go, the less likely your contract is to expire IN the money *(and you want you contract to be ITM when you close it out)*. Yeah, the further OTM you go, the cheaper the contracts get, but the extra risk isn't worth it to me. I usually aim for a Delta of .50 to .60 when I buy a contract *(which basically means between a 50-60% chance of the contract(s) expiring IN the money)*.

So back to the matter at hand- how does focusing on percentage over dollar amount help you keep a 'healthy' perspective about how much you should be satisfied with each day? Well, you can see that if you're only trading one or two contracts each day that cost between $100-$200, your daily P&L in dollars won't be that impressive. But that's OK, because your P&L in terms of *percentage* will actually be something you can be proud of.

2. Shift your focus from daily profits to weekly or monthly profits

If you're making $20 per day, that's nothing to really 'get excited' about when looked at in a vacuum. But if you make $20 per day for a whole week, suddenly you've made $100. And then if you're able to keep that up for a whole month, you realize you've made an extra $400 that month. Now, this is not the type of growth that will make you rich, but there's a LOT of things anyone can do with an extra $400 per month. When you stop focusing on relatively lackluster numbers like $20 per day, and start focusing on weekly or monthly gains, it can do a lot to improve your self-confidence and your excitement level about your trades.

CHAPTER SIX:
SELF-DECEPTION

Self-deception happens when you fail to see things as they truly are because of a willful rejection of the truth. While having a lack of perspective is more like *"you don't know what you don't know"*... self-deception is when you actually *do* know what you're doing wrong, but you refuse to accept it.

You'll probably notice a phrase I've repeated a few times in this book— failing to, *"See things the way they really are, rather than how you want them to be."* Self-deception happens when you fail to see your own shortcomings and faults—AND when you don't take credit for your wins.

People have all sorts of hangups. Sometimes, a person's ego is much larger than it deserves to be in relation to their actual achievements or skill level. But sometimes it's the opposite—and because of a lack of self-confidence or having low self-esteem, these people can't believe that they're actually *really good* at what they're doing, or that they *deserve to win.* This self-deception often leads to self-sabotaging behaviors.

Know yourself. A calm mind and a self-actualized mind is a powerful mind. I know it's impossible to be truly objective when assessing yourself, but you have to try. Don't be afraid to look in the mirror and tell yourself with *honesty* what you really see. Lay it all down on the table. The good, the bad… ALL of it. Criticize your shortcomings and celebrate your strengths. Figure out where you're strong, where you're weak… and take the actions you need to take in order to improve your weakest areas *(you're reading this book right now, so congrats…you're already doing it!)*

What are some signs that you're deceiving yourself?

1. Failing to acknowledge extended losing streaks

I believe most well-adjusted people are optimistic. But that natural optimism can become a problem if it overshadows other realities that you don't want to face. For example, if you have 4 days where you lose $100 per day, and then you have one $300 day, it's exciting to say, *"I made $300 today!"* But the fact is, even with your nice, green $300 day, you're still

NEGATIVE $100 on the week, which is obviously a problem.

The optimist in you wants to focus on your big win, but that's not helping you if it clouds your judgement to the fact that you're losing more than you're winning, even if the one individual win is bigger than any of the individual losses.

It's important to see 'the big picture' on many different time frames. Just like in day trading, where you combine the view on the 1-minute chart with the view on other time frames in order to see the big picture of that day's price action, you want to combine the view of your P&L on a daily basis with your P&L over a longer period of time. A three-day sample size isn't going to tell you much, but a 3 week or 1-month long sample size of your trading P&L will tell you a LOT more about your overall trading *in general*, giving you a more holistic view of how good or bad you're doing. You might have two out of three days be red and it's not a big deal. Two out of three *weeks* red is a much bigger problem.

2. Failing to take responsibility for your own actions

This is classic *"It's not my fault"* territory. Placing blame on a number of other things, or people, or situations beyond your control, rather than looking inwards to determine if YOU were in fact the cause of your failure. YES, luck is 'a thing'. There is GOOD luck and BAD luck. I'm not one of these people who says, *"EVERY single thing that happens to you is 100% YOUR fault"*. Sometimes, 'good' people simply find themselves in bad situations, and sometimes 'good' traders get unlucky. That's just life.

But there are times when your daily failures are *absolutely* your own fault. When examining a daily loss, you should always START by asking the question, *"What did I do wrong?"* And work backwards from there. If you start by looking for somewhere else to place blame, you'll never learn anything about yourself, because you're not taking responsibility for your actions. You'll never grow if you never acknowledge your limitations.

But when you do start with the idea of, *"What did I do wrong?"* Then you'll be hyper-focused on uncovering your own mistakes, therefore putting a microscope on everything relating to your trading style, and you'll be able to ask yourself questions like:

Was my technical analysis correct?

Did I let emotions get in the way of trading this correctly?

Was the timing of my entries or exits wrong?

Did I misread the charts and fail to identify a trend?

There are many more questions you should ask yourself, but these are just a few of the important ones. If you re-examine your entries and exits and come to the conclusion that you actually DID trade everything pretty solidly from a technical perspective, then it's time to look elsewhere and see if you really *were* just the victim of bad luck. Anything can happen during the course of a day.

For example, you might have a long position open on a ticker, and your analysis looks solid, the trend is there, and everything is actually working out. You're making money. Yay!! But then suddenly, in the middle of the day, the price falls through the floor within the span of a few minutes. What happened? It turns out the CEO of the company was just busted for fraud, causing the stock price to collapse. THIS is a textbook example of bad luck happening to you.

Nobody in the world *(outside a handful of federal agents)* would have known what was about to happen to this ticker. You could have had perfect analysis, and traded it perfectly based on your analysis, and you *still* would have lost in this particular case. This sort of thing is rare, but it *does* happen. And that's why it's so important to be able to analyze every losing trade to determine how much of the failure was *your* fault, and how much of the failure was due to forces completely beyond your control. And obviously, you don't want to beat yourself up over things you have no control over, but you DO want to do everything in your power to ensure that the actions that caused your failure don't repeat themselves.

3. Lacking the confidence to know when you actually know what you're doing

Self-deception goes both ways. Sometimes, you can be doing really well because of your own skill, and maybe because of a lack of self-confidence or an overabundance of humility, you chalk up all of those wins to having 'good luck' all the time. Failing to acknowledge your own skills can be as detrimental as failing to acknowledge your own shortcomings, because: just like how you want to *avoid* repeating mistakes, you want to *replicate* the behaviors that are giving you wins. If you always chalk-up your wins to 'good luck', that means you aren't taking credit for things YOU deserve credit for. And if you fail to see the things that YOU did right based on your own analysis *(not luck)*, then you don't know what to look for when trying to replicate that success.

Some exercises to help eliminate self-deception in your trading

1. Hold yourself accountable on a daily basis

A way to actually do this each day is: analyze every

trade as objectively as possible *(win or loss) and* try to determine how much of the success or failure was YOUR doing, and how much of it was due to forces beyond your control. Obviously, you want to note what those things are—and you want to repeat everything that's working and discard the things that aren't. This is definitely easier said than done, especially since no two trades are exactly the same, and sometimes moves that will work in certain circumstances won't work in others. This isn't an exact science. The point is—even though it's never going to be exact, it's still extremely beneficial to analyze your trades every day and try to identify all of your positive *and* negative behaviors.

Remember these 3 very important points:

Always hold yourself accountable for things that are your fault

Never beat yourself up over things that are *truly* beyond your control

Work on developing the ability to tell the difference between the two

If you really do take the time to analyze your trades each and every day, you'll not only learn about yourself, but you'll improve your trading through analysis. Simply putting in the hours, day after day, *will* improve your daily trading—as long as you're truly honest with your discoveries, positive *or* negative.

2. Force yourself to only consider longer time frames when judging your successes or failures

Like I've already said, considering just a few days' worth of trading results isn't enough to give you a holistic, comprehensive idea of how well *(or not)* you're doing. You can't have 2 or 3 green days in a row and think, *"I've cracked the code!"* And on the flip side, 2 or 3 red days in a row doesn't mean you'll 'never get it' and you should just quit.

If you're REALLY dedicated to learning how to do this for real, on a large scale—you need to look at longer time frames to determine 'where you're at', metaphorically speaking. It's much too easy to deceive yourself when you're only looking at a short time frame. If you're red 2 out of 3 days, you could say, *"I just had a slight hiccup"*. It's much harder to justify two red *weeks* out of three as a 'slight hiccup'. Therefore, to get the truest perspective—only judge your performance on longer time frames. This will force you to stay honest with yourself.

'Self-deception' literally means, *"lying to yourself."* NOTHING good can happen if you continue to lie to yourself. It can be hard to look in the mirror and be really honest with yourself, especially if you don't like what you see. But like I said—if you don't even know *what* to change, you'll never be able to determine *how* to change. Positive change is the point of this book. And it starts with being brutally honest with yourself.

CHAPTER SEVEN: COMPLACENCY

Of all the negative behaviors listed in this book, I think this is probably the least detrimental... but I still wanted to list it. Even though it might not be important to you *now*, it will become more important to you as you level up your trading.

Being complacent is not the worst problem to have, since this usually happens when things are going *well*. This is basically the manifestation of that old saying, *"If it ain't broke, don't fix it"*. But being complacent can definitely hurt you in the long run, because failing to develop your skills means you'll eventually start leaving profits on the table. If you're successful and you're happy making $500 per day... how much harder would it be to make to make 1K per day? Yeah, it will require more size, and the rollercoaster ups and downs will get a bit bumpier...

but it's not like you're in a different universe. The things you'd need to do differently are not *that* extreme. Just size up a little more and be a little more careful with your stops.

It's important to approach these changes with the right mindset. Intent and motivation are both very important in everything you do, whether it relates to dealings you have with other people, or in relation to yourself. And in this case, you don't want the motivation for sizing up to be *greed*, you want the motivation to be *self-improvement*. You're setting a goal for yourself, and you're challenging yourself to actually be able to do it. The extra money isn't the reward. Knowing you set a personal goal and *succeeded* in achieving that goal is the reward.

For me, the decision to scale up was never about saying, *"I'm not happy making $1,000 per day. I need to make $5,000 per day."* It was me saying to myself, *"How will I be able to handle the extra stress and pressure that I'll face when I scale up my trades?"* I looked at scaling up as an opportunity to set another, loftier goal for myself, and achieve it. The extra money was the result of *achieving the goal*. It wasn't the goal *itself*. Making more money was simply the result of being able to handle more pressure.

What are some signs that you're being complacent in your trading?

1. Failing to push yourself to the next level

When you stop pushing yourself you become stagnant. And by 'pushing yourself' I don't mean re-inventing the wheel. The strategy works, so stick with it. Don't feel like you need to change everything up *just because.* What I mean is: If what you're doing is working, keep doing that, but scale it. Don't be afraid to get out of your comfort zone and reach for that proverbial 'next level', whatever that level looks like to you. Throughout history, writers and philosophers have expressed variations of the idea that, *"If you fail to evolve, you die."* I agree with this wholeheartedly.

The beautiful thing about evolution is: we can all embrace it no matter where we're at along the path of our trading journey. Evolution can mean going from trading 1 contract to 2 each day, or it can mean going from trading one ticker each day to trading three per day, or it can mean going from making a 10% daily P&L to a 20% daily P&L. It can mean anything to anyone, and it's a personal goal that you set for yourself.

Whether or not you embrace these additional goals depends on your attitude. For ME, setting goals is FUN. I never look at it like, *"Oh shit, now I have yet another thing to worry about..."* I think of it as, *"I get to attempt to be an even better version of myself"*. Keeping an optimistic outlook in the face of setting new goals goes a long way towards being able to actually achieve those goals.

Everyone's motivation is personal. Find your own personal motivation and let *that* be your drive to improve.

2. Going on 'autopilot' rather than staying engaged on a daily basis

After you do this for years it can be very easy to 'disengage' and still be successful. There are days when I've slept late, turned on the computer 5 minutes before the open and still made 1K in 15 minutes, with no preparation or premarket study *(I do NOT condone this behavior)*. At this point, there's very little that surprises me on a chart. I *could* trade successfully with very little preparation, but I don't want to do that. I *want* to be prepared.

Not only does extra preparation help my success rate, but it also keeps me involved in the process. I don't want to just snap my fingers and make money— I want to feel like I solved some type of puzzle to make my money. And that's why I never like going on autopilot. Sometimes it will happen, but I really try hard to make sure it never does.

Going on autopilot can also hurt you in this way: when you've done the same thing over and over and it's just *kept working*, you might think you don't need to really pay much attention to detail because you'll think to yourself, *"This always works, so it will work again this time!"* Just last week I actually had some losing trades because of this exact thing, and it was an eye opener to me. I traded a few particular tickers in a way that's worked out for me about 90% of the time since the beginning of this year. If I had put more focus on *exactly* what I saw on the charts rather than thinking, *"This always works out when I trade it like this"* I would have traded differently and had winning trades instead of losing ones. I let myself get complacent, and it cost me. You see, even when we think we're on top of *everything*, it's easy enough to slip up at any time.

Some exercises to help keep you from getting complacent in your trades

1. Be habitually curious

Never stop learning. I have my strategy dialed in 100%, and I almost never have a red day. But I still constantly try to learn new ideas about trading. As I said in my first book, there are a million things you *could* learn about day trading and the stock market, and I only know a fraction of it. That doesn't stop me from being consistently successful, but I still want to learn about many different aspects of the market that I don't completely understand right NOW... and that's an example of being habitually curious.

I know that I don't necessarily *need* to learn anything new about trading, because I'm already successful. I just *want* to keep learning new things every day. And this goes beyond trading. As I write this, I'm attempting to learn Spanish. I'm constantly taking my photography skills to the next level. I play piano *(badly)* and I'm working on that. And on and on. Being 'an intellectual' doesn't mean having a Mensa level IQ. It means being excited about *learning for the sake of learning*. If you never stop learning, you never stop growing.

2. Don't take anything for granted

I just mentioned this briefly in my warning against 'going on autopilot'. When things are working, it's very easy to think they'll just *keep working*, no matter what. You might be able to get away with doing exactly the same thing each day for a while, but it won't last forever. For example, within the last year, the tech trade has been on fire. Tech stocks have been killing everything else. But just this week, tech stocks have sold off HARD. For months on end, you could wake up every morning and think to yourself, *"I'll just buy NVDA calls today at the open and close in the first hour and make a bunch of money"*... and you would have been right more often than not—until this week.

Your *strategy* should remain constant *(get in on the right side of the trend, ride the trend while it's working, get out before it reverses)* but the specific tickers you trade should be in a rotation based on what's working *right now*. I do have a handful of 'usual suspects' that I trade more than any others, but I do change out the rotation based on the big picture of what's working in the market at any given time.

CHAPTER EIGHT:
FEAR

Fear is the biggest problem for newer traders. It's easy to understand why, because when you 'don't know what you don't know', everything can seem scary. Fear keeps people from attempting greatness. Imagine if some of history's most consequential people had been motivated by fear rather than desire? They never would have attempted *(and achieved)* the world-altering things they did. You know the saying, *"Fortune favors the brave"* right? It's true in life, and I believe it's true in trading as well. DON'T let yourself become paralyzed by fear as you trade.

There are obvious fears, and hidden ones. I don't really need to go in depth about the obvious ones, because you already know what they are: being scared to enter the trade, being scared to use a big amount of size... things like that. But the hidden fears are the ones below surface level, and these can be even more detrimental in the long run. These fears are more about self-confidence issues. Thinking you'll never be good enough at this, thinking you'll never be able to trade like a professional, being afraid to give yourself permission to really *go for it* in your trading.

Of course, you need a certain level of skill and knowledge to start with before you do any serious trading. But once you DO actually know what you're doing *(knowing how to interpret price action, read candlestick charts, see valid trends setting up, etc.)* then at that point it's actually illogical to NOT enter a good trade when you see it setting up for you. Think about it like skydiving. Yes, the moment before you jump out of the plane it's extremely scary. But you have to *believe* that the parachute is going to open. You can't let your fear stop you from jumping.

Obviously, there's always the chance that any trade won't work. Nothing is guaranteed. But when you've done the work to prepare—you've studied the charts, you've set valid levels, and you see price cross the level that tells you it's time to enter… at that point there's nothing left to do but just take that leap of faith and enter the trade. The worst thing that can happen is you stop out for a loss, and you have a little bit less money than you had before. But if you're doing everything correctly, even when you have a loss, that loss won't be catastrophic, and you'll live to trade another day.

How MUCH preparation and self-confidence you'll need to build up before you let yourself get started or size up *(depending on where you're at in your journey)*... that's an individual thing that you'll need to determine for yourself. There's no 'magic number' of hours you need to practice until you say, *"I'm ready to start trading now."* The number is different for each person.

All I'm saying is—don't let an overabundance of fear paralyze you from doing this. Don't keep telling yourself, *"I'm just not ready yet"* when you actually ARE ready, but don't want to allow yourself to *believe* you are ready. There's a big difference between acting responsible and acting scared.

The *responsible* trader will be able to realize what they need to work on, work on those things, and then get to it after they know they've made the necessary preparations. The *scared* trader will never allow themselves to actually do what needs to be done, because they'll always find some excuse for it to NOT happen... a kind of 'self-sabotage' through fear.

What are some signs that you're trading scared?

1. You don't think that you have "what it takes" to

win.

I'm no psychologist, but I have met more than a few people in my life who seemed prone to self-sabotage. As soon as something starts going really well for them, they'll make some boneheaded decision and screw it all up. In trading, this most often presents in the form of a trader *drastically* oversizing/overtrading as soon as they achieve some small level of success. For example, they might be green trading small size for a few days or even weeks, and suddenly they think they've got it all figured out and say, "YOLO!" And trade SOOOO much bigger than they should. They will inevitably erase all of the gains they just made over the past few days or weeks in the course of ONE DAY when the trade goes against them, and they fail to exit from the position fast enough. Has this happened to you? I thought so. But don't worry- it's happened to me too, and yet here I am writing a book and enjoying a full-time career from day trading. EVERYBODY makes mistakes along the way. The ones who achieve consistent success are the ones who LEARN from their mistakes, stick with it, and don't make the same mistakes over and over. It's as simple as that.

2. You're hesitating too long before making a decision to enter

In order to be successful in day trading, you need to exercise quick, decisive action. Price action moves by the second, and sometimes one minute can make a huge difference in the price you get filled at. My strategy involves using market orders and not limit orders, so that means the fill price can vary. The longer you hesitate to make a decision, the more that price will fluctuate. That's why—when you see something setting up and you think to yourself, *"I should get in here"*… what are you waiting for? The longer you wait, the more danger you're putting yourself in as far as straying away from your 'ideal' entry point, second by second.

For example, let's say you've told yourself, *"Once price crosses above this resistance level I'm going to enter long."* Price then *does* indeed break through that resistance level. If your technical analysis was correct, then what *should* happen is—price should continue to pop, at least for a little while. If you get in right away once price breaks that level, then you're getting in while price is still AT the level, therefore giving you a comparatively lower price. But if you waited an additional 3 minutes… if your technical analysis was correct and price does continue to rise after it slices through the resistance level, then you'll end up paying more for the same contracts as you would have paid 3 minutes earlier. Most of the time, even a few minutes can make a huge difference in your fill price.

Many of us have experienced some of those

"imposter syndrome" feelings at some point along the way in our trading journey. Letting those imposter syndrome thoughts creep into your mind can also put fear into your trading. This actually happened to me when I was starting out. At first, I had a very optimistic *"fake it till you make it"* attitude *(with very little 'making it' early on in my trading career)*. NOW I am extremely confident in my abilities. I know that I know what I'm doing, and I know that my strategy just WORKS, nearly every single day. But there was an in-between period for a while after I first experienced consistent success, and I thought to myself, *"Is this just LUCK? Do I really know what I'm doing?"*

The sooner you can shake every bit of the imposter funk off of your aura, the better off you'll be. Of course, things won't go your way every day, but literally the FIRST STEP after you learn the skills of trading is to *believe you actually know what you're doing*. Don't internally fight it as you're outwardly exuding confidence. BELIVE IT FOR REAL.

Here's a statement I want you to contemplate for a minute: **ANYONE CAN LEARN *HOW* TO DO THIS, BUT NOT EVERYONE CAN *DO* THIS.**

What does that mean? The first half of this sentence means that the *learning* part of the process isn't that difficult. I mentioned this earlier in the book, and I'll reiterate it here: you don't need to have a

Mensa level IQ to understand what you're *supposed to* do. The amount of knowledge you need to amass isn't extraordinary. Sure, there's a definitely a learning curve, and you do need to do some studying up before you begin. But anyone of average intelligence can learn the skills and the steps they're supposed to take. But can you actually DO those things? That brings us to the second half of the sentence.

The fact is- not everyone has the amount of emotional discipline needed to actually *be* consistently successful. It's a lot easier to comprehend what you're *supposed* to do than it is to emotionally fulfill the promise of the strategy. You know that if "X" happens you should do "Y"… but when X *does* happen… will you actually *be able* to do Y?

This is where your ability to stay disciplined will come into play. As I mentioned earlier on in the book—for ME, starting out with a lack of discipline was my biggest *"Achilles heel"* amongst all the possible Achilles heels one might have. I've had to work really hard on this over the last few years. I can say I'm very disciplined in my trading now, but it was definitely work getting to this point. Understanding the charts and graphs and patterns and strike prices and expiration dates all came extremely quickly to me… but staying *disciplined* before, during and after trades was the biggest obstacle in the way of my becoming truly consistently successful.

If FEAR is your biggest Achilles heel, just train yourself to realize that this isn't a life-or-death situation. The stakes aren't as high as you're probably allowing them to become in your mind. It's NOT like jumping out of a plane. If your parachute fails to open, you die. If you lose in a trade, you've just lost some money. The only unseen monsters we're afraid of are the ones *we allow* to become terrifying in our minds. Trading is only 'scary' if you let it become scary.

Some techniques to keep you from being afraid:

1: Trade LOW PRICED options

I think we can all agree on this: if you asked 100 traders the question, *"What are you most afraid of in trading?"* Chances are, 100 of them would reply, *"I'm most afraid of losing money."* This is a logical fear to have. *Of course* none of us wants to lose money. But that brings us to a conundrum—this simple fact: no risk, no reward. You simply MUST overcome your fear of losing if you want any long-term consistent profits. You MUST accept some risk if you ever want to make 'real' money.

The good news is: if you're deathly afraid you'll lose a ton of money in your trades, simply trade VERY inexpensive contracts at first, even if they're on tickers that you aren't immediately drawn to. An example *(as of the writing of this book)* is INTC. It's not exactly a *"sexy"* stock at the moment, but it's also a *cheap* tech stock that also has a lot of volume and liquidity *(two things you definitely want when trading options)*. If you just want to practice your entries and exits with real money as opposed to paper trading, you could probably get 3 ATM options on INTC for under $100. This means, even if your contracts went to zero *(which they never will if you're trading correctly)* then the MAXIMUM amount you'd stand to lose would be $100. Even the biggest scaredy-cat in the world can deal with that, right? If you *can't* deal with that, you're probably not cut out to day trade options.

2. Start to *believe* in your technical analysis

There's a caveat to this one, and that is: you have to *know how to do* technical analysis first, before you can actually be confident in your analysis. But once you DO understand technical analysis, you need to start trusting it. Obviously no technical analysis is *always* right, but what we're doing is playing the averages here. If you just flipped a coin each morning to decide whether to go long or short on the day, you'd be right 50% of the time. But with solid TA, you can realistically up that percentage to 75%-80%. A 7 out of 10 chance that I'll be right is more than enough to get me into the trade. Once you know what you're doing and you believe in your skills, then get into the trades that you know are solid based on your TA.

CHAPTER NINE:
GREED

This is probably the most straightforward chapter in the book. Everyone knows what greed is, and everyone already has a good idea of how greed can negatively affect your trades. But giving in to greed goes much deeper than simply saying, *"I need more money!"*

The most obvious example of greed screwing up your trades is when you fail to take profits at the right time because you want to squeeze every single penny out of the trade, even when it becomes increasingly dangerous to do so. You *should have* walked away with your $300 profit on the trade, but instead you held on too long, and now your should-have-been $300 profit is $200, or even less. All because greed and hubris got the better of you.

The thing is—none of the negative behaviors listed

in this book exist in a vacuum. They're almost always accompanied by one or more of their co-defendants. For example, greed is often accompanied by too much competitiveness or a lack or perspective— the trader *needs to win bigger than anyone else* at all costs, and that dogged determination makes the trader lose sight of what's actually happening right in front of them.

Having 'big dreams' and a vivid imagination are both beautiful things. You wouldn't be reading this book right now if you didn't have both. I know you've already imagined how perfect it would be to have giant green trades every single day, raking in hundreds or even thousands of dollars a day in less than an hour. This IS possible! I know, because I do this nearly every day. But don't ever let those big dreams cloud your judgement to the point where you lose your place in space.

And what do I mean by 'place in space'? It simply means—be realistic about what's possible at that moment based on the information/experience you have, and the size of your account. For example: if you won't be happy unless you make thousands of dollars per day with a $500 account and you've only been trading for a month… you have lost your place in space. A trader with one month of experience under their belt and a $500 account *should be* extremely happy to make $20-30 per day.

I still remember my first REALLY BIG win... one that I *(for all practical purposes)* had nothing to do with. I can't even remember which ticker I was trading—just some random ticker I had read about somewhere *(this was back when I read as much as I could about different tickers to trade, because I had no idea what I should actually be trading)*. I had NO technical analysis skills, NO ability to read charts, NO real trading knowledge of any value... but I wanted to be a day trader so badly I just followed anyone who seemed 'legit' and aped their trades, jumping in on whatever tickers these 'professionals' were hyping.

So, some online trader said to go long on whatever ticker it was, and I jumped in with a few contracts. I didn't spot a good place to exit that day, so I held overnight. The next morning when I woke up, I discovered the stock had gapped up, and my contracts had made me about $1,600 overnight. I didn't even understand what gaps were, how they worked or how I was supposed to trade them... nothing. I DO remember just about having a heart attack when I saw my account balance that morning.

Did I think that the same thing was going to happen every day? HELL no. At least I understood my 'place in space'. I realized I had gotten extremely lucky, and I didn't assume the same thing would be happening regularly. The difference between then and

NOW is that—I'm an actual professional with real skills now. I can make thousand-dollar days happen nearly every day now and know that it's ME making it happen—no luck needed. But back *then*... that particular trade was 100% GOOD LUCK. I can't take any credit for that one.

The point of this story is that- even though I had the incredible 'beginners' luck' trade, I didn't think that I could replicate that result day after day, because I understood my place in space. I'm not a greedy person, so I didn't think that I had to make $1,600 every day in order to feel 'successful'. And because I DIDN'T succumb to any sort of greed, I was perfectly OK with going back to making $20, $30, $40 dollars a day after my blockbuster $1,600 day. You can see where I'm going with this. Had I been lured by greed into thinking, *"$20 a day isn't good enough"* at that particular time, I would have altered my trading style to be MUCH more reckless and riskier in an attempt to re-capture that lighting in a bottle. And that would have ended badly.

RIGHT NOW, of course $20 a day isn't good enough for me. But I'm in a completely different place in space now than I was back then. It's extremely important to be honest with yourself about the stage of your development, and trade accordingly. Where you'll be at a year from now is NOT where you are now. Don't trade based on where you think you'll be next year. Trade based on where you're at NOW.

What are some signs that you're trading greedy?

1. Never being satisfied with the size of a win

A win is a win. Yes, *obviously* we want all of our wins to be *massive*. But you need to learn how to appreciate small gains. As with anything you do *(doesn't matter what it is)*, you never start at 'Apex level'. There's always a learning curve, preparation, training, etc. Doesn't matter if it's preparing to run a marathon or graduating college or learning a new language. There's always a progression involved in getting where you ultimately want to be. You must be OK with small wins at first, knowing the *bigger* wins will come later. The bigger wins WILL come, as long as you progress correctly and avoid the major pitfalls along the way.

The level of win you should be satisfied with will change based on where you're at in your journey. For me right now, a $100 daily win isn't something that excites me. Yes, of course every win is great, but it's not *exciting* to me now because of where I'm at in my journey. But when I was first starting out—making $100 per day for multiple days in a row was *extremely* exciting. If you are a newer trader, don't think that

$100 per day is 'not enough'. Focus on your *progress* over the daily P&L.

2. Failing to take profits on big pushes because you want to see even larger P&L

When price suddenly breaks hard in your favor on a trade, that's a gift to you. Take advantage of your good fortune, snatch up the gains while they exist, because they could be gone at any moment. I can't tell you how many times I stayed in too long because I wanted *just a little bit more* out of the trade, even when all the signs were telling me I should get out. I don't do that very often now, but I used to. With experience comes wisdom.

Just remember this: when you have a big push happening in your favor, that's REAL profit that you can snatch up right NOW with the click of the mouse. Sure, obviously you could wait it out and maybe squeeze even more profit out of the move before it reverses on you... but it could ALSO fall out hard at any second and wipe out whatever gains you've just made in the last 10-15 minutes.

What I like to do is close out approximately 80-90% of my position size fairly quickly after a big move happens to lock in my profits but leave a much smaller amount *(10-20%)* open just in case the price does keep going in my direction for longer than expected. That way, I get the best of both worlds: the security of making a decent profit right now, and the possibility of making a much bigger profit on that smaller number of contracts later on.

The 'smaller for longer' position size takes some risk out of the equation, because even if price reverses on me, I have already locked in profits from closing a majority of my contracts already. To leave ALL of your contracts open as long as possible in the hopes of a huge, sustained move is not only greedy, but also ineffective in most situations.

What are some techniques to keep you from trading greedy?

1. Focus on PROCESS OVER PROFIT.

Focus on the process first, and the profits will follow. Greedy people only think about money. A greedy trader will almost always eventually end up being one *(or both)* of these:

1. Broke

2. Unsatisfied

If you have a greedy nature—then even when you are successful, you'll be more prone to missing out on feeling the joy of your success, because your success will *never be enough*. And what's more—if you're trading greedy, you're more likely to give up all of your gains when the trade reverses on you, because you'll hold on too long trying to make back the lost gains. You'll end up looking like Gollum, with every single dollar being, *"My precious!"*

As I mentioned above—you can close out a majority of your contracts early and just leave *a few* open if you want to try to play both angles—that way you'll lock in profits quickly and have a very small position size that can *possibly* make you more over time.

2. Force yourself to take profits

I know it's easy to think that when a trade is working, it's just going to keep working. But NO trend lasts forever. Every stock chart resembles waves in the ocean... rising, falling, rising again. The first step in successful trading is learning how to interpret the candlesticks and chart patterns and let them tell you where price is *probably* going to head next. The next step is taking action to lock in the profits when you have them. I've had plenty of trades that I looked at in hindsight and said to myself, *"Man, if I had just held it open a bit longer, I would have made a lot more"*... but you know what? I've had even MORE trades that I closed just before a big reversal happened, because the charts told me it was getting dangerous to stay in, and I closed my positions when the danger got too close. I was able to do that because I'm not greedy.

If I were a greedy trader, then I'd always be trying

to hold out longer and longer to squeeze out just a few more dollars on every trade… and the more you do that, the more danger you put yourself in. Force yourself to take profits when the charts are telling you that the trend might be running out of steam. Even if you don't make as much as you *wanted* to make on any particular trade, accept the gift you've been given. There's always the next one, and the one after that.

CHAPTER TEN:
GLUTTONY

When I say *"gluttony"* I basically mean *"overtrading."* This can happen whether you're green or red on the day. Perhaps you're up and you think the trend you're riding will last forever. Or perhaps you're losing, and you think that by 'revenge trading' you can make up everything you just lost. You need to set targets for both the profit level you desire and the level you'll stop out at if the trade goes against you. If you ignore these levels, you're showing a lack of discipline.

Gluttony on green days is basically GREED, and gluttony on red days shows a lack of discipline, an over-competitive nature, a lack or perspective, or all of the above. Gluttony can also appear in the form of you NOT understanding the proper sizing. As a general rule, I never like to get into more than 20% of my TOTAL amount of contracts at one time. What this means is- for example, if I'm planning on trading a maximum of 50 contracts TOTAL on that day, then I would never let myself have more than 10 contracts OPEN at any one time. So, if I DID have 10 contracts open, I'd wait until I closed a few before I re-entered again.

This 'in and out' approach ensures that I can stay nimble. If there's one sudden unexpected move against me, I'm never too deeply stuck in the position. If I do close for a loss, then that loss is less than it would have been if I were holding more contracts. And if I want to make my *other* possible move *(which is hold on if I think there's a reversal coming)* I am also in less danger since my position size is smaller. This is the equivalent of the 'stick and move' technique in boxing. In one contract, out one contract. In one, out one. And on and on until I've traded the maximum amount I want to trade for that day. Seeing price move in your direction and immediately jumping in with huge size all at once is being gluttonous.

What are some signs that you're exhibiting gluttony in your trading?

1. When you have so many tickers going at once that you struggle to keep track of them all.

As a rule, I try not to trade more than 2 or 3 tickers

max at any one time. Anything more than 3 tickers and you simply cannot keep track of price action with the focus that's required. You need to study the movement of the candlesticks for each and every trade you have open, so if you have 10 trades open at the same time, how can you possibly focus on each chart? You can't. I've tried to trade 5 or 6 tickers at once before, and it just doesn't work. Sure, theoretically you could make money trading a bunch of tickers at once... I mean, anything is *possible*... but the practical reality is, you just can't pay close enough attention to anything more than 3 at a time, so save yourself the headache and the money—and only trade between 1-3 different tickers at any one time.

2. When you get too deep into your pool of capital each day.

Whatever size your trading account is, NEVER trade 100% of it in one day. What this means is—for example: if you have a total of $3,000 capital, don't buy 10 contracts that each cost $300 in one day *(therefore maxing out your account)*. Make sure you leave yourself some cash reserves just in case those trades don't work and you need to close for a loss. Everyone knows the old saying *"live to fight another day."* This is what you're doing when you leave yourself enough capital in your trading account. Even if you have a losing day, when you don't go 'all in' each day, then that one losing day doesn't wipe out your account. Therefore, you can *"live to trade another day."*

What are some ways you can combat gluttonous trading?

As with so many other chapters in this book—the solution to most of the problems you'll face on a daily basis is simply to set rules for yourself. It's no different here. When you trade in a gluttonous manner, it's a bit like going to the all-you-can-eat buffet when you're really hungry. Your eyes glaze over at the sight of all the delicious food, and you want to eat it ALL, right NOW. But you know that if you give in to that urge to eat *everything* now, you'll pay for it later—either in the form of a food coma or an upset stomach. But if you make yourself slow down and relax—if you take your time and eat what you want, but *responsibly*… you'll enjoy the buffet AND you'll feel happy and satisfied when you're finished.

You can trade anything you want, all day every day. There's no need to rush. It's not like there's 'one plate of options' and if you don't get there first there won't be any left for you. It's easy to understand why a trader *(especially a newer trader)* would want to jump in with too much, too soon. Trading IS exciting. It's an adrenaline rush when things are going your way, and it's terrifying when they don't *(which is its own type of rush, just not a*

GOOD one). But once you've been doing this for a while you'll see that good trading isn't like throwing everything at the wall to see what sticks... it's carefully and methodically choosing what and when to trade. Trading well is like shooting a sniper rifle, not a shotgun.

So, back to setting rules in regard to eliminating gluttony. The two most important limits you can impose on yourself to help eliminate gluttonous trading are:

1. Never trade more than 3 different tickers at any one time

2. Never trade with more than 20% of your capital each day

Now, rule number one is an absolute rule. Anything more than 3 contracts at once is simply not ideal. But rule number 2 is open to interpretation. Some people advise not to trade with more than 3% of your overall capital each day... which is great if you have $100,000 in your trading account. But for MOST retail traders who have somewhere between $2,000 to $20,000 in their account, 3% on the day isn't giving them enough to work with to actually make a real profit. If you've got $5,000 in your account, 20% of that is $1,000. And trading with $1,000 per day is *definitely* enough to make you $100 or more each day when you're trading well. Sometimes I will use more than 20% of my capital in one day, but that's rare. I'll need to see something really promising in order to take the extra risk of going larger with my size.

CHAPTER ELEVEN:
TRACKING YOUR PROGRESS

Now that you've started to identify and eliminate self-sabotaging behaviors in your day trading, now what? The next step is keeping track of your progress over time. I'm going to explain the best way to do that in this chapter.

If you read my first book, *'Secrets of the Lone Wolf Trader',* you know that I've been practicing the Martial Art of Muay Thai for over a decade. One of the things I love about Martial Arts so much is that it puts you on an endless path of *searching* for perfection, while at the same time understanding that it's impossible to actually *achieve* 'perfection' *(and you must be OK with that fact).*

Trading is very similar. It's extremely rare to have what I would consider to be 'the perfect trade'. It has happened to me a few times in my life, but it's rare... and more importantly, I'm not getting hung up on 'perfection', I'm simply trying to be better today than I was yesterday, and better tomorrow than I was today. That constant quest for self-improvement is one of the many things I love about day trading.

I love knowing that even though I'm consistently successful and have been for years, there's always something new I can learn. Something new I can try, some slight variation of my strategy that I can experiment with. I DO believe in that old saying, *"If it ain't broke don't fix it"*, so none of the 'tweaks' I make are anything more than that… just *slight* tweaks. My core strategy remains the same: **Identify a valid trend, get in on the right side of the trend, and ride the trend while it lasts, taking profits along the way… and get OUT of the trade by the time the trend strength starts to wane.**

But even though this core strategy is something I never stray from, there are subtle variations I can make, and this is one thing that keeps it feeling 'fresh' every day, even though I've done essentially the same thing for years now.

At this point I have basically conquered my trading demons on the grand scale, but I'm FAR from perfect… so paying attention to my daily trading habits and trying to perfect those habits as much as possible is yet another way I keep myself in a constant state of evolution. The journey is NEVER over. The main goal is simply to make that journey as 'correct' as possible, day after day.

One thing I talked about in *'Secrets of the Lone Wolf Trader'* was the importance of identifying your own motivation. What's the REAL reason you want to be a day trader? Is it the money? The freedom? The social flex? It can be any one of those, or many others— and there's no 'right' or 'wrong' answer here. It's just good to know where your head's at, so-to-speak. When you're able to honestly identify your own motivations, it becomes easier to understand your own strengths and weaknesses, and the reasons those strengths and weaknesses exist.

For example, someone who simply fetishizes money above all else might be more prone to GREED than someone who prioritizes living that 'finance bro' life and being able to tell everyone they're a full-time options trader. *That* person might be more prone to experiencing self-deception or over-competitiveness. Of course these are just broad generalizations, but you get the point. MY problem was always feeling TOO free, the *"I do what I want, when I want"* attitude… and that's why a lack of discipline was *my* Achilles heel. Luckily, I was able to see that, and take the necessary steps to fix it.

Now that we're reaching the end of the book—if there's ONE thing I'd like you to take away from this book, it's this: **KNOW YOURSELF.** I've tried to give you different techniques you can use to not only identify but also correct various negative behaviors you might have while day trading. The more you know yourself, the more honest you can be when identifying and interpreting your own true strengths and weaknesses. And that's all I'm trying to do here... help you *know yourself* better.

Getting back to what I said in the beginning of this chapter: tracking your progress. How do you do that? It's actually pretty simple. First of all—you should have *already* been logging your daily P&L each day... if you haven't started doing that, start immediately. How will you identify any improvements if you have no baseline to start from? Once you have amassed a few weeks or months of daily data to look at, AND you have identified your own personal hangups... then it's time to employ the techniques in this book and determine if they're helping.

For example: let's say you suffer from overtrading, and you always find yourself in a hole because you trade with larger size than you should *(gluttony)*... try the technique of ONLY allowing yourself to trade 3 to 5 contracts total each day. MAKE yourself do this each day for a few weeks. Track your progress each day, just as you were doing before. The total dollar amount of your profits and losses will go down *(because there's simply less gains OR losses from trading 3 contracts than there are from trading 30)* but if you're staying disciplined, your percentage P&L should go up *(your winning P&L percentage should get bigger, and the P&L on your losses should get smaller).*

Another example: maybe you suffer from greed, and you've noticed that you always give away a good chunk of your profits by mid-day, because you can't keep yourself from trying to squeeze *just a little more* out of a trade, even when you can see that the trend is losing steam and may reverse on you soon. Give yourself a hard profit target, like, *"When I make X amount of money, I WILL close all of my contracts."* Hopefully you will see that after you start doing this, even though your highs won't be as *dramatically* high, in total you'll come out in better shape because you'll have more days making 10%, rather than a few days here and there making 20% while having a lot of 2% days *(because you stayed in too long and lost your gains).*

The good news in all of these situations is: you're always evolving as a person AND a trader, and that means you'll never run out of new milestones to strive for. Just because you may scale things back to 'get a grip on yourself', that doesn't mean you can't go big again *after you do* get a grip on yourself. Size down and trade conservatively until you've proven to yourself that you're ready to go back to trading with as much size as you were using before.

Think about yourself like a professional athlete: athletes train SUPER hard, but if they get an injury, they scale back their training considerably until they've healed... and *then* they get back to training as hard as they did before once that injury has healed. Just like a stock chart never goes in a straight line, neither does your progress. You'll find yourself killing it sometimes, and possibly going into extended losing streaks at other times *(it happens to everyone)*. Never get too drunk on your wins, and never get too bummed out over your losses.

When you track your progress over the longer term, you'll see more of the 'big picture' view of how you're doing. I've already said it multiple times in this book—don't judge your progress simply by looking at your day-to-day P&L. Stretch it out. Look at your week to week or month to month P&L. The shorter your time frame, the smaller your sample size. And the smaller your sample size, the less holistic your view will be. Anyone can be green for 4 days straight. But can you be green for 4 *weeks* straight?

There's an extremely simple method to determine if your P&L is trending in the right direction: just keep track of your daily P&L and then add up your daily gains or losses into one weekly total at the end of the week. Do this each week and compare the weeks to each other. Once you have amassed a few months of data, compare the months. Always put more importance on your monthly trend than your weekly trend, and more importance on the weekly trend than the daily trend. Maybe the third and fourth week of this month you were down from the first & second week of this month. But was this *month* better than last month? If so, then you're trending in the right direction overall, even if your most near-term P&L has dipped a little bit.

CHAPTER TWELVE: PUTTING THE PIECES TOGETHER

Here we are at the end of the book! I'm certain that what you just read was easy enough to understand… but will you be able to put these concepts into practice on a daily basis? That's on YOU. The one thing I always tell beginning traders hoping to make this a full-time career is:

It's easy enough to *learn how* to do this. It's a lot harder to actually *do* this.

As I said earlier: you don't need a genius level IQ to know what you're supposed to do when you look at the chart. But can you *actually do* those things? That's the whole point of this book. Identifying all those pesky little self-sabotaging behaviors that keep you from consistency.

Like I said in the beginning of the book, making money day trading isn't hard. Achieving *consistent* profits *IS*. We're all trying to be as 'perfect' as we can be every day. If you weren't striving for day trading perfection you wouldn't be nearly finished reading this book right now.

That vision of 'perfection' might be the most intoxicating muse you'll ever chase. But remember, there is no 'absolute' perfection. No day will come when you wake up and say to yourself, *"Well, that's that! I've cracked the code. I have achieved day trading perfection."* It's an endless daily grind. Each morning you need to wake up having a sharp, focused, and optimistic mindset. Literally EVERY SINGLE DAY I truly *believe* to the depths of my soul that I WILL make money that day. Of course, I don't make money *every* single day, but I've got roughly an 80-90% success rate, and that's fine with me. The most important part is not setting yourself up to lose before you even begin.

I really do believe that most of the problems you'll face along the way in your trading journey will be mental and emotional in nature rather than intellectual, meaning—you won't make bad decisions because of a lack of comprehension or information—you'll make bad decisions because your emotions prompted you to make those decisions, even though you DID know what you *should have done* in many situations.

There are plenty of times in the past when I knew what I should have done based on what the chart was showing me, but some internal hangup prevented me from actually doing the thing I *should have* done. **DOING THE THING YOU KNOW YOU *SHOULD* DO** in any given situation. That's the ultimate goal in day trading. Even when a move doesn't work out—as long as you did what you know you should have done, you can sleep well at night with your decision.

The only time I 'beat myself up' over a trade is when I DON'T do the thing I know I should have done. I never make a trade without doing technical analysis on a chart before getting involved. When I do my usual preparation and make my move based on sound technical analysis, with my emotions under control—if that trade doesn't work out, I don't stress about it.

Remember that umbrella analogy from a few chapters back? When you make the right moves based on sound technical analysis and still lose… that's essentially you getting caught in a downpour even though there was only a 20% chance of rain. It WILL happen sometimes. If you lose while taking a *calculated* risk, that's never something you should stress out over. But if you lose because you took unnecessary, *reckless* risks—THAT'S when you need to stop and check yourself before going any further. You might not have been able to tell the difference between the two before reading this book, but hopefully you do now.

The last thing I'll say before wrapping this up: although there's no absolute 'right' or 'wrong' way to trade, you need to ask yourself: What does trading *mean* to you, and what do you need it to *do* for you? Your answers to these questions will shape the way you trade. If you answer honestly, you can formulate a trading style that works for you.

For example: in my case, day trading provides my entire income. I'm not playing around. I trade large size, and I accept more risk for the possibility of more reward. It wasn't always like this for me: when I started trading, I still had a full-time job, and I slowly 'graduated' into being a full-time day trader once I realized I could make a LOT more money doing this in a fraction of the time. I didn't 'choose' day trading… it chose me. I would have been a complete fool *(or a masochist)* to ignore the opportunity to make 3X the yearly salary while "working" about 1-2 hours per day.

My style of trading is very different from the hobbyist who just wants to dip their toes in and trade 1 or 2 contracts per day just to see what happens, without even really worrying about the outcome—or the person who uses trading as a 'side hustle' to supplement their income. I *need* to get more out of my trades each day, and that's why I trade with large size, and why I'm OK with accepting a bit more risk for more reward.

Remember, the temptations that might develop could change based on what style of trading you're doing. For example—if you trade with really large size, you might be more prone to fear creeping in, because every little fluctuation in price action is magnified when you're using large size. You can quickly watch a small loss become a BIG loss, and that could *(obviously)* scare the shit out of you.

On the flip side, if you're only trading small size, you might be more prone to experiencing greed or a lack of perspective. Obviously, we all want to make as much money as possible each day... but when you're trading one contract you need to be realistic about how much profit you can actually squeeze out of that one contract. You might say to yourself, *"I need just a little bit MORE..."* letting that greed take over because you're not happy with making $50 on the day *(which will most likely be your reality when you're trading 1 contract per day)*... and then before you know it that $50 profit is suddenly a $50 loss because you didn't get out when you should have.

This basic idea of determining a *need* for your trading *(and therefore a trading style)* is not so different from what you'd hear from an investment advisor. They ask you questions like, *"What's your time frame? Are you looking to generate income, or simply invest? Do you need immediate access to your cash, or not?"*

Are you looking for day trading to provide 100% of your income, or less? Do you *want* to transition into doing this full time someday, or are you happy keeping your day job and just approaching your day trading like a fun hobby or supplemental income? All of these things matter when you're developing your own personal trading style.

Of course, this is a broad generalization—but I believe that if you want your trading to provide more of your total income, then you need to be OK with accepting more risk and using bigger size. I know this runs contrary to what many people think. I've heard it said over and over, *"Managing risk is the most important aspect of trading"* and I generally agree with that statement—but remember, there are *calculated* risks and then there are *reckless* risks. The person who wants to make day trading their full-time income needs to be OK with taking on *calculated risks*.

Out of ALL of the countless numbers of successful trades I've made in my lifetime, I'd guess that in at least 50% of them, at some point I was RED on the trade before I eventually closed it out GREEN. Very few trades go perfectly from open to close. In simple terms, what this means is: if I had closed every trade the second I went red on that trade, I would be one of those unsuccessful traders who lost all their money. I know you've heard the horror stories: *"Only 1-10% of traders can actually be consistently successful!"* I don't know what the *exact* number is, but I would agree that an overwhelming majority or traders DO lose more than they win. But YOU obviously want to be in that 1 to 10% club of winners. One of the ways to actually get there is to avoid overtrading and avoid trading scared. The main goal is not just *"live to fight another day"* but *"WIN, day after day"*. When you trade scared, you'll never be able to take any calculated risks. And without calculated risks, your profits will always be average at best.

Now, there's nothing *wrong* with being average. If you're looking at day trading like a 'side hustle' or a fun hobby, and you don't want to put too much money into it, then a very modest 2% daily P&L for $20-50 bucks might fit you perfectly! I'm personally writing from the perspective of a full-time trader relying on trading to provide 100% of my income. If I was writing this from the perspective of a hobbyist, my tone of voice and advice would be different. But you can take the knowledge and exercises from this book and make it work for your trades, whether you're trading 1 or 100 contracts per day. If you can simply identify your psychological strengths and weaknesses, and then do real work on your weaknesses, I truly believe your trading WILL get better over time.

Remember: a calm mind is a happy mind, and a happy mind is a successful mind. If you can wake up every day and like what you see when you look in the mirror, you're winning. And wherever you're at in your journey, I believe that with the right combination of knowledge, discipline and mindset, you CAN be successful in day trading, swing trading, and longer-term investing.

I hope you enjoyed this book, and I wish you many green days to come. If you'd like to get my complete options day trading video course and learn all of the exact techniques I use to trade each and every day, you can find it at www.lonewolftradingclub.com. You can also find my first book, *"Secrets of the Lone Wolf Trader"* on Amazon if you'd like to get the complete 'nuts and bolts' strategy guide behind my specific trading strategy. Thanks again for reading this book, and good luck!

About the Author

Patrick Buchanan is a full-time stock options day trader, musician, photographer and citizen of the world. He's lived on 3 continents and visited over 30 countries, and currently splits his time between the US, South America and Southeast Asia.

In addition to writing about day trading, he also conducts private online coaching sessions to teach traders his strategy 1-on-1.

In his free time, he writes and records music, tours with various bands, trains in the martial art of Muay Thai and creates fine art and fashion photography. You can purchase his complete options day trading video course at: www.lonewolftradingclub.com

www.ingramcontent.com/pod-product-compliance
Lightning Source LLC
Chambersburg PA
CBHW071937210526
45479CB00002B/715